TO ZACH.

HAPPY BIRTHDAY

WITH LOVE FROM

G. UNCLE PAUL &
G. AUNT KAREN

ANN ROSSI

Bright Ideas

The Age of Invention in America
1870–1910

NATIONAL GEOGRAPHIC

Washington, D.C.

PICTURE CREDITS

Cover U.S. Department of the Interior, National Park Service, Edison Historical Site, page 1 Museum of the City of New York/CORBIS; pages 2–3, 8, 21 (top), 25, 26, 27, 29, 33, 34, 35 (bottom), 39, 40–41 Brown Brothers, Sterling, PA; page 4 (inset), 16, 30 Smithsonian Institution, Washington, DC; pages 4–5, 8 (bottom background), 19, 37 (bottom), 38 Library of Congress; pages 6, 7 Lynn Museum, Lynn, MA; page 9 US Patent Office; page 10 © Levi Strauss & Company Archives; page 11 Breton Littlehales/ National Geographic Society; pages 12 (top), 15 (bottom), 20–21, 23, 37 (top) The Granger Collection; page 12 (bottom) Rob Boudreau/Stone; pages 13, 14, 20 (top), 22, 32, 35 (top), 36 Culver Pictures, NY; page 15 (top, left) The Western Reserve Historical Society, Cleveland, OH; (top, right) Photodisc; page 17, 24 (top), 33 (inset) Archive Photos, NY; page 18 Property of AT&T Archives/Reprinted with permission of AT&T; page 23 (inset) Grant Heilman Photography, Lititz, PA; page 24 (bottom, left) Gaslite Advertising Archives; 24 (bottom, right) International Museum of Photography at George Eastman House; Breton Littlehales; page 28 Keystone View Co/FPG; page 31 Art by Arthur Lidov/National Geographic Society, Image Collection.

QUOTATIONS

Page 4 From *Those Inventive Americans,* edited by Robert L. Breeden (Washington, DC: National Geographic Society, 1971), p. 132. Page 7 From *Always Inventing: A Photobiography of Alexander Graham Bell,* by Tom L. Matthews (Washington, DC: National Geographic Society, 1999), p. 60. Page 16 "A Lady in a Machine Shop," an interview in *Woman's Journal,* December 21, 1872, as quoted in *Feminine Ingenuity: Women and Invention in America,* by Anne L. Macdonald (NY: Ballantine Books, 1992) p. 51. Page 28 From *The Inventing of America,* by Bruce Norman (NY: Taplinger Publishing Company, 1976), p. 151. Page 32 From *The Wright Brothers: How They Invented the Airplane,* by Russell Freedman (NY: Holiday House, 1991), p. 66.

Library of Congress Cataloging-in-Publication Data

Rossi, Ann.
  Bright ideas : the age of invention in America, 1870–1910 / by Ann Rossi.
      p. cm. — (Crossroads America)
  Includes index.
   trade ISBN: 0-7922-8276-0
   library ISBN: 0-7922-8356-2
  1. Inventions—United States—History—19th century—Juvenile literature. 2. Inventions—United States—History—20th century—Juvenile literature.
  [1. Inventions—United States—History—19th century. 2. Inventions—United States—History—20th century.] I. Title. II. Series.
   T21.R56 2005
   609.73'09'034—dc22

                                        2003019834

Produced through the worldwide resources of the National Geographic Society, John M. Fahey, Jr., President and Chief Executive Officer; Gilbert M. Grosvenor, Chairman of the Board; Nina D. Hoffman, Executive Vice President and President, Books and School Publishing.

PREPARED BY NATIONAL GEOGRAPHIC SCHOOL PUBLISHING

Ericka Markman, President, Childrens Books & Educational Publishing Group; Steve Mico, Senior Vice President & Editorial Director; Marianne Hiland, Editorial Manager; Anita Schwartz, Project Editor; Tara Peterson, Sam England, Editorial Assistants; Jim Hiscott, Design Manager; Linda McKnight, Art Director; Diana Bourdrez, Anne Whittle, Photo Research; Matt Wascavage, Manager of Publishing Services; Sean Philpotts, Production Coordinator; Jane Ponton, Production Artist; Susan Kehnemui Donnelly, Children's Books Project Editor. Production; Clifton M. Brown III, Manufacturing and Quality Control.

PROGRAM DEVELOPMENT

Gare Thompson Associates, Inc.

BOOK DESIGN

Steven Curtis Design, Inc.

NATIONAL GEOGRAPHIC SOCIETY
1145 17th Street, N.W.
Washington, D.C. 20036-4688

Printed in Mexico

TABLE OF CONTENTS

"There is no substitute for hard work.
Genius is 99 percent perspiration and
1 percent inspiration."

~*Thomas Alva Edison*

Introduction

Imagine a world with no lights or no telephones. What if you could not travel by car or airplane? How far could you go? With no electricity, work would be harder. You could not run your computer, or the washing machine, or the TV. Without inventions, life would be very different.

Many things we take for granted today, such as telephones and gas-powered cars, were invented during the Age of Inventions. From 1870 to 1910, new machines and new ways to do things changed the way we lived and worked.

Inventors found ways to improve products. They dreamed up new ones. Some inventions were never used. Others, such as the electric lightbulb, changed the world.

CHAPTER 1

Inventive Minds at Work

Between 1870 and 1910, many inventive minds were at work in the United States. Inventors came from a variety of backgrounds. Some, such as Thomas Alva Edison, were born in the United States. Others, such as Alexander Graham Bell, were **immigrants**. Some had a college education. Others had little or no schooling.

What did these people have in common? As inventors, they were curious, creative, and good at solving problems. They did not give up easily. They worked through a problem until they solved it. They had the right resources, knowledge, and tools to produce their inventions.

Jan Ernst Matzeliger used his inventive mind and resources to invent a machine that revolutionized the way shoes were made. He had come to the United States in the 1870s. He came from Dutch Guiana (now Suriname), a country in South America. He worked for a shoe manufacturer in Lynn, Massachusetts. While working, Matzeliger noticed that it took a long time for a worker to attach the top part of a shoe to the sole. This work, called lasting, was done by hand. The best workers could last at most 50 pairs of shoes a day. Matzeliger was sure he could invent a machine that could do the job much faster.

| Jan Ernst Matzeliger

Matzeliger worked for four years to develop a working model of a lasting machine. Then he worked for years to perfect it. Often he barely ate. He spent his food money on things he needed to improve his machine.

Finally, in 1883, Matzeliger received a **patent** for his invention. A patent gives someone the right to be the only one to make, use, and sell a new invention for a certain period of time. His lasting machine made shoes ten times faster than a skilled worker did. It cut the cost of producing shoes in half. As a result, shoes became cheaper. More people could afford to buy them. However, lasters were now out of work. A machine did their jobs.

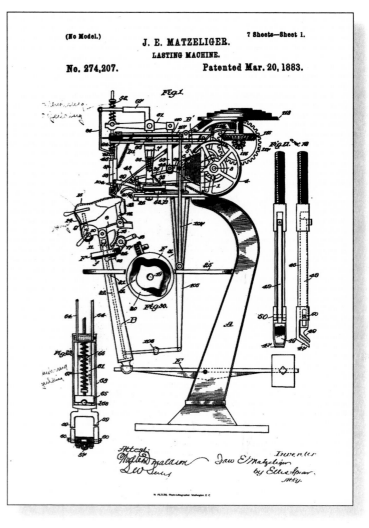

(No Model.)   J. E. MATZELIGER.   7 Sheets—Sheet 1.
                            LASTING MACHINE.
No. 274,207.   Patented Mar. 20, 1883.

Why Do Inventors Invent?

Jan Matzeliger wanted to find a better and faster way of doing things. Other inventors are just curious. Some just want to make money. Still others want to make people's lives safer or more fun.

Andrew Jackson Beard, an African American, wanted to make rail work easier, quicker, and safer. Beard worked in an Alabama rail yard. He saw many workers get injured when they were connecting railroad cars. A man had to wait until two cars came together and then connect them with a heavy pin. Sometimes a man's hand or arm was smashed between the cars when they came together.

Beard worked hard to invent an automatic way to connect railroad cars. In 1897, he received a patent for the Jenny Coupler. It was a device that let railway cars be joined automatically. The use of Beard's invention probably saved many workers from being hurt.

Meet Leo Hirshfield

Leo Hirshfield was one person who did his best to sweeten America. Hirshfield was an Austrian immigrant. He came to America with a recipe for chewy, chocolate candy. In 1896, he produced the first batch of his special candy. He named it Tootsie Roll® in honor of his five-year-old daughter. Her nickname was Tootsie.

HOW DO INVENTORS MAKE MONEY?

Inventors who want to make money from their inventions need to patent their invention with the government. The patent gives a person or a company the right to be the only one to sell a product or a method for doing something for a certain number of years. With a patent, no one else can make or sell the invention without the inventor's permission. Sometimes more than one person comes up with the same new product or method. The first person to get a patent for it owns the invention.

Not all patented inventions make money. Take a look at this invention. Can you guess why it never became a best-seller?

S. S. Applegate received a patent for this device to wake a person.

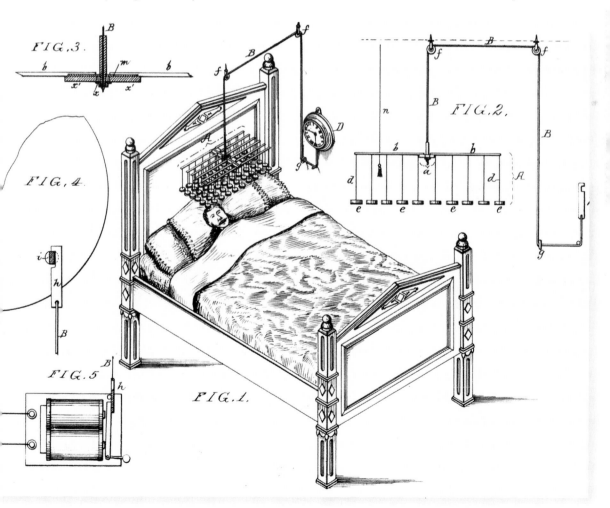

What Makes an Invention Successful?

A successful invention appeals to many people. Some inventions solve problems. Others improve ways of doing things. Still others promise a better and easier lifestyle. Some inventions—such as Coca-Cola® and Levi's® jeans—are more than a hundred years old. Yet, they are still popular today.

Another very successful invention was created more than one hundred years ago. It was Elijah McCoy's automatic lubricator. McCoy received more than 50 patents for his inventions, which included a lawn sprinkler and tires. The automatic lubricator was probably his most important invention. It allowed small amounts of oil to drip automatically onto the moving parts of a machine while it was in use.

Before McCoy's invention, people needed to stop machines to oil them by hand. Otherwise, the engines could break down or become too hot and catch fire. Using McCoy's invention, people no longer had to stop work. McCoy and his invention saved people time and money.

Meet Levi Strauss

In 1873, Levi Strauss and Jacob Davis invented a new kind of pants. They sewed metal rivets, or bolts, onto pocket seams. These bolts made pants last longer. The pants were a big hit in the West. Miners loved them. They could put gold nuggets and rocks in their pockets. Their pants would not tear! Today, people all over the world wear jeans.

CHAPTER 2

Overcoming Obstacles

Inventors face many challenges. Some have trouble finding the right materials. Others have trouble solving a problem. At times, inventors run out of money. They have to stop their work. Sometimes, two or more inventors are in a race. It is a race to see who gets the patent first.

Some inventors spend time protecting their inventions. There have been many legal battles over inventions. A lot of money was at stake. Thomas Alva Edison had many legal battles with other inventors who tried to claim his inventions.

Laboratory of Thomas Edison in Menlo Park, New Jersey

MAKING INVENTIONS WORK

Often, inventors spend a long time trying to solve a problem. They spend years trying to find the right materials to make an idea work.

The lightbulb took years to perfect. Most lightbulbs burned out too quickly. They lasted only minutes. Edison and his team tried hundreds of materials to find one that would last a long time. They tried paper, cotton thread, fish line, wood, and metal. They even tried threads from a spiderweb and strands of hair from a beard! Edison himself said, "The electric light has caused me the greatest amount of study." Finally, they found a material that worked. It was carbonized cotton sewing thread.

Inventors often need a long time to reach their dream.

The incandescent lamp invented by Thomas Edison used carbonized thread to produce light. Today, neon is often used in electric lamps and signs.

- The Wright brothers wanted to fly. They spent over seven years studying and experimenting before Orville Wright made the first successful airplane flight.

- Leo Baekland experimented for five years before he created Bakelite®. It was the world's first hard plastic that was able to resist heat. Bakelite was a success. It was easy to mold. It was used to make telephone receivers, handles for pots and pans, knobs, and other things. Bakelite helped make Baekland a wealthy man.

MEET ORATOR WOODWARD

Jell-O® has been a popular dessert for nearly 100 years, but it wasn't always a success. The person who owned the patent for Jell-O didn't have much luck selling his product. He sold the patent to Orator Woodward. At first, Woodward didn't have much luck selling Jell-O either. Sales were so bad that he tried to sell the patent for $35. No one bought it. Then, in 1902, he advertised Jell-O in *Ladies' Home Journal*. He called it "America's Most Famous Dessert." Four years later, Jell-O was a million-dollar seller.

COMPETITION

For years, the **telegraph** was the fastest way of sending a long-distance message. Unfortunately, only one message could be sent at a time. People wanted faster communications. Inventors set to work to find ways of sending many messages at once. Alexander Graham Bell was one of those inventors. He and his assistant, Thomas Watson, worked hard to produce a multiple telegraph, but inventor Elisha Gray beat them to it.

Bell had another chance to beat Gray. This time it was for what many called a "speaking telegraph." Working into the night, Bell and his **draftsman**, Lewis Latimer, prepared Bell's application for "Improvements in Telegraphy." It was filed on February 14, 1876. It was filed just a few hours before Elisha Gray informed the U.S. Patent Office that he was working on a device that could send speech. Luck was with Bell the second time around. He received the patent for an invention that became known as the telephone.

Stages in the Development of the Telegraph

First form of key

Improved form of key

Early relay

First Washington-Baltimore telegraph

OVERCOMING OBSTACLES

Prejudice was a huge obstacle that earlier inventors faced. African Americans were **discriminated** against, or treated unfairly. Many were not allowed to get a good education. They had little choice but to educate themselves. They read books and studied after work. Inventors like Lewis Latimer, Granville T. Woods, and Garrett Morgan worked in fields such as communications, transportation, and engineering.

Lewis Latimer became an expert in the lighting industry. He was a self-taught draftsman, drawing plans and designs. After helping Bell with his patent, he became interested in electricity. Latimer helped build the first electric plants in Philadelphia, Montreal, and New York City. He helped open a lightbulb factory in England.

While working for Thomas Edison, Latimer wrote a book that explained electricity. His inventions included an improved electric lamp. He also created an early version of an air conditioner.

New York's first central electric power plant, Pearl Street Station, 1882

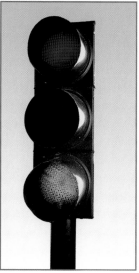

Modern-day traffic lights are modeled after traffic signals invented by Garrett Morgan.

Granville T. Woods has been called the "Black Edison." He patented more than 50 inventions. Woods was an experienced engineer and had gone to college. Still, he could not get the jobs he wanted because he was African American. So, Woods decided to work for himself as an inventor. His Synchronous Multiplex Railway Telegraph (1887) allowed conductors and engineers on moving trains to send and receive messages. They could be told if another train was in their path. As a result, many train accidents were avoided.

Granville T. Woods

WOMEN AND DISCRIMINATION

Women also had to overcome discrimination. Many people believed that women could not understand math or science. They thought that women could not invent things. In fact, women were not allowed to patent inventions until 1809.

Many of the inventions women patented between 1870 and 1910 were designed to help other women. These inventions made work in the home or on the farm easier. Anna Corey Baldwin invented a milker that shortened the time needed to milk a cow. Margaret Knight received her first patent in 1870 for the device shown below that cuts, folds, and pastes paper bags.

Women also invented products, devices, and methods that were used by businesses and industries. Amanda Theodosia Jones, for example, invented a vacuum canning process. She used this process to open a canning company.

CHAPTER 3

Building a Brighter America

Between 1870 and 1910, many inventions changed America. They changed the way Americans worked and lived. More railroads and highways were built. People and goods could get from place to place faster. The telephone made it easier for people to communicate and to keep in touch with family and friends.

The electric lightbulb lit up homes, businesses, and city streets. Cities grew tall as the first skyscrapers were built. The last American frontier was fenced in. Household appliances gave people more **leisure** time. Americans found new ways to amuse themselves.

Luna Park in Coney
Island, New York

THE TELEPHONE

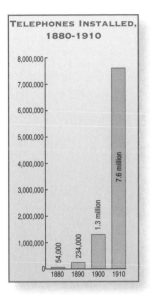

TELEPHONES INSTALLED, 1880-1910

8,000,000			
7,000,000			
6,000,000			
5,000,000			
4,000,000			
3,000,000			
2,000,000			
1,000,000			
0			

54,000 — 1880
234,000 — 1890
1.3 million — 1900
7.6 million — 1910

In 1876, America celebrated its hundredth birthday. It held a Centennial Exhibition in Philadelphia. One of the inventions shown at the Exhibition was the telephone. Soon, Alexander Graham Bell was demonstrating his invention around the world. He even gave a private demonstration to Queen Victoria of England. Like others, she was amazed that she could talk to someone who was miles away.

Queen Victoria wasn't the only one who wanted a telephone. Many others did as well. By 1877, the Bell Telephone Company was formed. Soon, telephone poles were raised, and wires were strung up. Telephone exchanges opened in cities across America. By 1892, phone service began between New York and Chicago.

Bell's invention amazed people. But then, Bell was an amazing man. He became an inventor when he was 11. A friend's father challenged him to do something useful. So, Bell invented a tool that removed the husks from wheat kernels. Bell was also interested in speech and communication and taught deaf and mute students. On March 10, 1876, after experimenting for years, he succeeded in sending the sound of the human voice across wires. He spoke his first phone message to his assistant, Thomas Watson. He said, "Mr. Watson—Come here—I want to see you."

Alexander Graham Bell demonstrates his telephone.

The number of Americans who owned phones skyrocketed. When people first began using the telephone, many yelled into it. They thought they had to yell to be heard at the other end.

The telephone replaced the telegraph as the fastest way to communicate long distance. A telegraph message had to be sent through an operator. Then it was delivered as a letter. The telephone allowed people to have direct conversations. It changed the way people conducted business. It brought rural and urban America closer together.

The telephone also brought new job opportunities for women. The first telephone operators were boys, but they were often rude to customers. Women soon replaced the rude boys. They were considered much more polite.

MEET EMMA NUTT

Emma Nutt was the first female telephone operator. She was hired in 1878. For many years, women who worked as telephone operators had to

- be very proper.
- be unmarried.
- have long arms to reach the top of the telephone switchboard.
- work ten or eleven hours, six days a week.
- ask permission if they wanted to go to the bathroom or get a drink of water.

AMERICA GLOWS

Can you imagine what life would be like today if Thomas Alva Edison hadn't invented the electric light? And he didn't stop there. He wanted to bring electricity into every home and business in America. So, in 1882, Edison and his associates opened the first electric power plant in Manhattan. As the demand for electricity grew, power stations were built in other communities.

Edison's business was inventing. He enjoyed solving problems even as a child. As he grew older, this desire to solve problems became his life's work. In 1876, he built the first research lab in the world in Menlo Park, New Jersey. He hired researchers to solve problems and invent new products. Edison was known as the Wizard of Menlo Park. He received 1,093 patents from the United States patent office—more than any other inventor! Among his inventions were the incandescent lamp, the phonograph, and the first practical motion picture viewer.

| Thomas Alva Edison

AMERICA USES ELECTRICITY

Edison had many competitors. One of them was George Westinghouse. He and his staff developed a device that sent electricity over longer distances. By the late 1880s, Westinghouse was also busy lighting up America.

Electricity changed the way people worked, lived, and played. Businesses installed electric lights. Now people could work at night. Electric lights lit up the streets. People could walk more safely after dark.

Electric companies made more money when customers used more electricity. Therefore, companies wanted people to use electric appliances. Inventors created electric washing machines, sewing machines, and vacuum cleaners. Ads boasted that electric gadgets were easy and fast to use. People bought them.

| **An early electric vacuum cleaner**

Soon electric streetcars replaced horse-drawn trolleys. (Trolleys were like our buses.) Electric **vehicles** became the main way of getting around in cities. In the 1890s, an electric trolley system allowed many Philadelphians to move away from the city center. Now, people could live far from the city and ride the trolley to work.

CITIES GROW TALLER

Cities were being wired for electricity. They were being connected by telephones. Cities were changing in still other ways as well. They were growing taller.

The first skyscrapers were built in Chicago in 1885. They replaced some buildings destroyed in the Chicago fire of 1871. Construction workers used steel frames, new tools, and machinery to build taller buildings. Soon, skyscrapers were springing up in New York City. More people could work and live in taller buildings. Cities grew larger. Streets became more crowded as people rushed to and from work.

Skyscrapers could not have been built without elevators. No one would work or live in a tall building without an elevator. It would take too long to walk up and down hundreds of stairs! Luckily, elevators had been invented years before the first skyscrapers were built.

In the early 1800s, many people were afraid to use elevators. Elevators often crashed to the ground. In the 1850s, Elisha Graves Otis invented the safety elevator and demonstrated it to a huge crowd. People watched as he went up in his elevator. Then his assistant cut the rope that kept the elevator up. The crowd gasped! The elevator did not crash. Otis convinced people that elevators were safe to use.

The 22-story Flatiron Building in New York was completed in 1902.

SETTLING THE LAST FRONTIER

New inventions also changed the West. Farmers used improved plows and machinery to plant crops on larger areas of land. The railroad moved people and products across the country.

Two major problems faced settlers on the Great Plains. One was not enough water. Settlers needed water for themselves, their crops, and their animals. Windmills solved the problem. In the 1870s, settlers began to use improved windmills to get water. The windmills pumped water from deep underground to the surface of the earth. Now crops could grow even in dry periods.

The second problem on the Plains was a lack of wood. Settlers needed wood to build fences. They wanted to keep their animals safe, but hardly any trees grew on the Great Plains. At first, settlers planted thorny shrubs as fences. The thorny shrubs inspired the invention of barb wire. Joseph Glidden's barb wire was easier to use than thorny shrubs. It was also a cheap, popular replacement for wood fencing. Railroad companies used the wire to keep cattle off the tracks.

Barb-wire fences and windmills became common sights on the Great Plains.

LEISURE AND ENTERTAINMENT

Thanks to inventions, Americans in 1910 had more time to relax than ever before. Better transportation meant people spent less time getting from place to place. New gadgets and machines made chores faster and easier to do. People had more time for fun. They went to amusement parks. They rode the Pleasure Wheel, today known as the Ferris Wheel. People played phonograph records and listened to music. They watched movies and took photographs. They went for drives in the country in a Model T, America's most popular car at the time.

They also enjoyed going for bicycle rides just for fun. Bicycle racing became popular.

George Ferris built this wheel for the World's Columbian Exposition in Chicago in 1893.

Americans were enjoying other sports, too. Baseball, football, and basketball became popular. James Naismith invented basketball in 1891. He had been asked to create an indoor winter sport. The goals were wooden peach baskets. By 1893, metal hoops with net bags replaced the peach baskets. By 1913, the nets were open at the bottom, just as they are today.

MEET GEORGE EASTMAN

"Almost a Kodak."

$5.00

The New No. 2
Folding Brownie

George Eastman developed his photography hobby into a successful business. He invented the first lightweight, affordable camera. It was the Kodak box camera. Anyone could use it. Its slogan was, "You press the button. We do the rest."

CHAPTER 4

America Takes to the Road

Before the car, people walked or bicycled. They rode on horses, in horse-drawn carriages, on trains, or on electric streetcars. Cars, however, gave people more freedom. People used them for business and for pleasure. Cars opened up new markets for businesses. Cars took people and goods farther and faster than a horse, bicycle, or streetcar could. With a car, people could explore new places. They could visit family and friends who lived far away.

The automobile brought problems as well as benefits. It dirtied the air. It was noisy. It made city traffic worse and caused accidents. Even so, America fell in love with cars.

MASS PRODUCING THE CAR

Before the 1900s, cars were handmade. It took a long time to make one. They were expensive. In the early 1900s, car manufacturers began to **mass produce** cars. Factories used **standard,** or the same, designs to make large numbers of cars. Mass production cut down the time and money needed to make a car.

In 1904, Henry M. Leland of the Cadillac Automobile Company began building cars that used **interchangeable** parts. Each car of the same model used the same kinds of parts.

A year earlier, in 1903, Henry Ford had opened the Ford Motor Company. Ford had worked as an engineer for Thomas Edison's company, the Edison Illuminating Company of Detroit. He left the company to build automobiles. He had already built two in his spare time!

Henry Ford and the first Ford automobile

At one time, Ford considered mass producing cheap watches. However, he realized he'd have to sell more than 600,000 watches to make a profit! Instead, he decided to mass produce cars. He could make fewer cars and make a bigger profit. He would make the cars cheap enough so that most people could afford to buy them.

At first, Ford's factory produced only a few cars a day. The price of these cars was high. In 1908, Ford's company put the Model T on the market. As production became more efficient, manufacturing costs dropped. Ford passed some of the savings on to his customers. Lower prices helped make the Model T a big seller.

Assembly line in an early Ford factory

Model T cars and electric trolleys create a traffic jam.

In 1910, Ford opened a large factory in Highland Park, Michigan. He wanted to make cars faster. The factory used standardized and interchangeable parts. Each worker did just one job. In 1913, Ford perfected mass production by adding a moving **assembly line** to the process. Cars rolled off the line! The price of the Model T dropped from $500 in 1913 to $440 in 1915 and $290 in 1924.

VOICES FROM AMERICA

"A scientific discovery's a fine thing in itself but it doesn't help the world till it's put on a business basis."

~ *Henry Ford*

CHAPTER 5

The Sky's the Limit

For thousands of years, people had dreamed of flying. Some had taken to the air in hot-air balloons or in **gliders,** planes without engines. But it wasn't until 1903 that a person flew. That year Orville Wright flew in a gasoline-powered, heavier-than-air machine near Kitty Hawk, North Carolina. The flight lasted only 12 seconds. It traveled just 120 feet. It was the first of many flights by Wilbur and Orville Wright.

When the Wright brothers were 7 and 11, their father gave them a toy helicopter. A twisted rubber band attached to twin propellers made it fly. The boys played with it until it fell apart. Then they built other toy helicopters. Larger ones didn't fly as well.

The Wright brothers stopped experimenting with flight, but started again when they were older. In 1903, they became the first people to build and fly an airplane. Five years later, they produced the world's first practical passenger plane.

EARLY FLYING MACHINES

The Wright brothers were not the first Americans interested in flying. In 1894, Hiram Maxim built a huge, heavy, steam-powered flying machine. It crashed. Samuel P. Langley built small model airplanes powered with steam engines. Langley thought that if his model airplanes could fly, then a full-sized version would, too. In 1896, Langley built a steam-powered wooden model airplane. It flew about one-half mile in almost a minute and a half. Then, in 1903, he built a full-sized gas-powered version of his model. He called it the *Aerodrome*. Twice the *Aerodrome* was launched from the roof of a houseboat. Both times the *Aerodrome* fell into the water.

After lifting off from the top of a houseboat, the *Aerodrome* nosedived into the Potomac River.

THE WRIGHT BROTHERS EXPERIMENT

The Wright brothers learned all they could about flying. They read about other people's experiments with flying. They wrote letters to people who had tried to fly.

The brothers also watched birds. They noticed that birds changed the position of their wings as they flew. Birds used their wings to keep their balance and control the direction of their flight. The Wright brothers reached a conclusion. Their glider would have to fly like a bird. They would have to be able to adjust the glider's wings to control it as it flew.

After nearly three years of studying, the brothers built their first glider. They flew it near Kitty Hawk, North Carolina, in 1900. Their goal was to learn how to control the glider and keep it balanced.

For nearly two years, the Wright brothers worked on problems with lift, or take off. Sometimes, they doubted they ever would

The Wright brothers experiment with their glider.

fly. But they kept trying to solve their problems. They built a wind tunnel. They experimented with differently shaped wings. They used what they learned to design and build a machine that would fly. In the summer of 1902, they made hundreds of glides in the wind tunnel. After making adjustments to the tail, they were ready to build an airplane.

FLIGHT!

First, the plane needed a light, powerful motor. Such motors did not exist. The Wrights and a friend had to make it. Next, the brothers had to make the rest of their plane, but there was a problem. They couldn't build the plane in their shop. It was too big! It would have to be put together in Kitty Hawk.

By December 14, 1903, they felt ready to fly. They assembled their plane, *Flyer*. Wilbur would go first. He climbed onto *Flyer*. The plane took off, stalled, and crashed into the sand. Luckily, Wilbur was unhurt. The plane had lifted only a few feet. Even so, the plane was slightly damaged. They fixed it. Three days later, it was Orville's turn to try flying. The plane had a slow start. Suddenly, it was in the air! *Flyer* was flying! It was a short flight, but it was successful.

Glen Curtiss designed this early plane called the *June Bug*.

Hardly anyone noticed the first flights. Wilbur and Orville kept improving their planes. By 1908, they had signed a contract with the Department of War to make the first military airplane.

The brothers also got a contract from a European company. The company wanted to make Wright *Flyers*. In 1908, the brothers gave their first public flight demonstrations. Wilbur flew in France. Orville flew in the United States. Suddenly, the Wright brothers were famous! The age of flight had truly begun.

CHAPTER 6

Inventing the Future

T he Age of Inventions changed life for many in America. People left farms and moved to cities. Cities became busier, noisier, and more crowded. Building became an important industry.

Telephones, cars, and airplanes made the world seem smaller. It became easier and faster to keep in contact with people and to get from place to place. Improved communications gave people faster ways of getting information.

Electric lights brightened streets, homes, and workplaces. They turned night into day. Electric-powered appliances made chores quicker to do. They gave people more time to do other things. Inventions, such as the phonograph, telephone, and the typewriter, created new jobs. More women started working. Factories hired workers for jobs on assembly lines.

BETTER, FASTER, CHEAPER

Not surprisingly, cafeterias and fast-food restaurants began to appear. They satisfied people who wanted to save time and money. People could walk into a restaurant and in minutes have a hot meal for just pennies. They didn't have to spend hours peeling, boiling, baking, or cleaning up! Mail-order businesses increased in number, too. They gave people who lived in the country an easy way to buy things. They were also convenient for people who had no time to shop.

A Woolworth's 5- and 10-cents store in New York City in the early 1900s

More department stores also appeared. As factories produced more and cheaper goods, **chain stores** developed to sell them. F. W. Woolworth began as one store in 1880. By 1900, there were 59 stores. Now, consumers could buy the same new products, such as vacuum cleaners, electric irons, and other labor-saving machines in any store in the same chain.

MORE JOBS

More and more people wanted to buy popular inventions. So, factories had to make more of them. Factories needed more supplies to make more goods. Industry became more important than ever.

A delivery truck (1915)

Take a look at the car. Many products are needed to manufacture a car. Metals need to be mined and **processed**. Rubber has to be collected from rubber trees. Then it needs to be processed. Glass, tires, paint, and other car parts must be manufactured. Factories need to order supplies. Materials must be shipped to factories. Workers need to make parts. Finally, the cars must be put together. Making a car takes many workers.

Jobs don't end once a car is made! The car still needs to be sold. Advertisers write ads. Some ads are printed in newspapers. Some are played on the radio. A salesperson sells the car. A car needs gas to run! It needs to be filled up at a gas station. And one day it may need repairs. Cars create jobs for advertisers, salespeople, gas station attendants, and mechanics. Delivery people, traveling salespeople, ambulance drivers, and others use cars in their work, too. It's easy to see how one invention creates many jobs.

A gas station in the early 1900s

New Kinds of Jobs

Many inventions created new jobs almost immediately. As telephones became popular, they had to be manufactured. Telephone lines had to be strung up. Operators had to be hired. Phones needed to be repaired.

Inventions also led to new kinds of jobs. For example, the success of the airplane created jobs in a new field called **aviation**. It also led to new kinds of jobs in construction, travel, and the military. Stunt pilots performed daredevil tricks. Military pilots gathered information about enemy forces. Airplanes carried soldiers and supplies to wars.

Passenger airlines began flying. Airports were built. Flight attendants were hired to care for passengers. Travel agencies sold tickets and tours. Planes delivered mail and goods. Mapmakers took photos from the air. They used the photos to make maps. Today, airplanes do all these things and more. They carry water to put out fires. They water and fertilize crops. Ranchers even use planes to count livestock!

AMERICA CHANGES

As new inventions became a regular part of American life, they caused other changes. With more people owning cars, the highway system spread rapidly. More paved roads were built. Many families moved to the **suburbs,** where a car was necessary.

One of the greatest changes new inventions brought was increased leisure time. By 1900, baseball had become the national pastime. Listening to records became popular. Then in 1906, Reginald A. Fessenden made the first radio broadcast that included music and the sound of the human voice. Families began to spend their evenings listening to the radio. Some radio programs became extremely popular, especially baseball games!

A family listens to records played on an early phonograph.

37

Many inventions amazed people. The airplane was awe-inspiring. Few people would have dreamed that one day airplanes would carry people around the world or that a spacecraft would reach the moon. Often one invention leads to another. The invention of the telegraph, for example, led to the invention of the telephone and radio. Photography inspired the invention of movies.

Edison's invention of a motion picture device that used a roll of film led to the development of movies and television.

Sometimes, inventors used ideas from more than one invention to make something new. Movies and sound recording were combined to create talking pictures. The invention of the telephone, radio, and movies led to the invention of television. And all of these inventions led to the development of the computer and modern ways of communicating.

Before the 1900s, most inventors worked alone. Then, Thomas Edison set up the first research lab in the United States. Now, most inventions take place in a research lab. What will inventive minds create in the years to come? One thing is certain. They will use the tools that inventors of the past have given us.

GLOSSARY

assembly line – a line of workers and machines used for putting together a product step-by-step in a factory

aviation – the science of designing, building, and flying aircraft

chain store – one of a group of stores owned by one company

discriminate – to treat unfairly

draftsman – a person who draws plans or designs

glider – a very light aircraft without an engine that flies by floating and rising on air currents

immigrant – a person who comes to live in a country in which he or she was not born

interchangeable – able to be switched or used in each other's place

leisure – time to do what one likes

mass produce – to make large quantities of identical things in a factory

patent – a legal document giving the inventor the right to be the only one to make, use, or sell a new invention for a specific period of time

prejudice – a negative attitude or opinion based on a person's or group's race, religion, or other characteristic

process – to prepare by some special method

standard – something that is accepted as a model

suburb – an area on or close to the outer edge of a city

telegraph – a device for sending messages over long distances by wire or radio

vehicle – something in which people or goods are carried from one place to another

INDEX